ALL-STARS

by John Fawaz

SCHOLASTIC INC.

ISBN 978-0-545-36767-7

© 2013 by NBA Properties, Inc.

Published by Scholastic Inc.
SCHOLASTIC and associated logos are trademarks and/or registered trademarks of Scholastic Inc.

12 11 10 9 8 7 6 5 4 3 2 1   13 14 15 16 17/0

Designed by Cheung Tai
Printed in the U.S.A.   40
First printing, January 2013

CONTENTS

Kobe Bryant soared into the NBA in 1996. Brimming with talent, confidence, and the drive to be his absolute best, Kobe was a great athlete. But he was not yet a great player. He still had a lot to learn.

Kobe progressed rapidly by studying the NBA's biggest stars and spending countless hours practicing and training. When he made his first trip to the NBA All-Star Game in 1998 as a guard for the Lakers, he was well on his way to becoming a superstar.

"I just want to be the best basketball player I can be," said Kobe. "If that happens, that will be fine."

Kobe has made that dream a reality and is now one of the best players ever. In his first 16 seasons, from 1996 to 2012, he helped lead Los Angeles to seven appearances in the NBA Finals and

five championships. He received the 2007–2008 NBA Most Valuable Player Award, and in 2011–2012 he earned his tenth All-NBA First Team selection. He finished the 2011–2012 season with 29,484 career points, the fifth-highest total in NBA history.

In addition, Kobe is one of the most popular professional athletes in the world. His jersey is an NBA top seller globally, and Kobe has traveled internationally to promote the NBA and its charitable causes. In Beijing, China, fans cheered loudly for Kobe as he led the United States to a gold medal in the 2008 Olympics.

"We thought we had some popularity over here, until Kobe came," said Carmelo Anthony, Kobe's teammate in Beijing. "They are just excited to see him over here."

In 2012, Kobe again hit the international court, helping lead the USA to another gold medal win at the London Olympics.

Meanwhile, back in the NBA, Kobe is still driven to be the best. At the 2011 NBA All-Star Game, his 37 points, 14 rebounds, and three steals led the West to victory in Los Angeles. He also received his fourth NBA All-Star Game Most Valuable Player Award.

"He's been here a long time, but he's still playing like he's 22 years old," said Oklahoma City Thunder forward Kevin Durant. "As a player, you can only hope and pray for a career like he's had."

CHRIS
PAUL

At 6 feet tall, Chris Paul is usually the shortest player on the court. Not that he minds. It's always been that way. Chris grew up in North Carolina playing against his older brother, C.J. The games began in the living room with a mini-hoop. Soon they moved outdoors to a homemade court built by their father, who gave Chris his very first basketball. "I was probably around five years old," said Chris. "I was playing in a recreation league. You feel like you're big business now, you feel like a trooper when you have your own basketball. You don't have to go to the gym and wait for someone to miss a shot so you can shoot the ball. You have your own."

Chris may have been younger and smaller, but he received no special treatment from C.J. and his friends. Those games taught Chris a valuable lesson: Size was not nearly as important as attitude.

"You just have to be aggressive," Chris said. "That has always been the case in basketball—the person who is the most aggressive almost always wins. That's the way it's always been for me."

Almost from the beginning, Chris dominated the older kids. His quickness allowed him to get to the hoop against even the tallest players. And whenever the defense clogged the middle, he would shoot from the outside.

His dad helped him develop into a complete player. "My dad was my coach," Chris said. "He knew that I could score in bunches, so he made me pass the ball and run down the court, get ready, and get the rebound. Therefore, if they miss, then I can score. That's where I think I get my pass-first mentality."

Professional teams recognized Chris's talent, too, and in 2005 he was selected to play for the New Orleans Hornets. On the court, Chris would face players who were often a foot taller than he. Yet, he still dominated. During his first four professional seasons, Chris won the NBA Rookie of the Year Award (for 2005–2006) and earned All-NBA First Team honors (in 2007–2008).

A knee injury cut short Chris's fifth season in 2009–2010. Though he returned in 2010–2011, he struggled at first. As he regained full strength in his knee, his aggression returned. By season's end, he had reclaimed his position as one of the best point guards in the NBA, and then he began a new chapter in his career when the Hornets traded him to the Clippers. Chris earned All-NBA First Team honors in 2011–2012 while leading Los Angeles to its first playoff appearance in six years.

"We had a good season," Chris said after the Clippers lost to the Spurs in the 2012 Western Conference Semifinals. "I think it's a good sign for our team, but there are no moral victories. . . . We're going to keep working. We've got some work to do."

As a toddler, Kevin Durant stood out—literally. He was the tallest kid in his class and did not like the attention. He always felt like everyone was looking at him. But at age seven, he began playing basketball. That's when everything changed.

Kevin fell in love with the game, so much so he told his mother that he wanted to grow up to be a basketball player. To help Kevin reach his dream, his mother, Wanda Pratt, worked the late shift at the United States Postal Service and signed him up to play for an Amateur Athletic Union (AAU) team near their home in Washington, D.C. His coach was his godfather, Taras Brown. Kevin's mother and godfather could see Kevin was very talented at playing basketball. But they also made sure he did his homework and his chores every night.

One day, before Kevin's team made a trip to North Carolina for an AAU tournament, Taras gave his godson an additional homework assignment. He had Kevin write "Hard Work Beats Talent When Talent Fails to Work Hard" over and over, on four pages of paper, front and back, before he would let him play in the tournament.

From then on, Kevin lived by that motto. He had great talent; everyone could see that. But Kevin didn't just rely on his talent alone. He worked hard, constantly practicing and pushing his own limits. That was lesson number one.

Lesson number two came when Kevin was 15. He had become a confident player. Maybe *too* confident. Before an AAU tournament game, Kevin exchanged trash talk with an opposing player, promising to score a lot of points against him. In the game that followed, Kevin's opponent dominated while he played horribly. It was the last time Kevin ever made that mistake.

"That made me mature," he said in 2010. "It made me respect everybody's game, and that pushed me over the top."

Kevin went on to become one of the nation's top high-school players and then a star at the University of Texas. He had grown to 6-9, with long arms that gave him the reach of a much taller player. But he also had the speed and shooting ability of a guard, making him an all-around strong player.

The Seattle SuperSonics chose Kevin with the second overall pick in the 2007–2008 NBA Draft, and he went on to win the 2007–2008 NBA Rookie of the Year Award. After the season, the

Sonics franchise moved to Oklahoma City and was renamed the Thunder. Kevin averaged 25.3 points per game in 2008–2009, and then led the NBA in scoring in 2009–2010 (30.1 points per game), 2010–2011 (27.7 points per game), and 2011–2012 (28.0 points per game). This made him a three-time NBA scoring champion. Even though the Thunder lost to the Heat in the 2012 NBA Finals, many experts predict that Oklahoma City will be the NBA's next great team.

Kevin has grown into a superstar. But his godfather's words still echo in his head. Every time he thinks about taking a day off, or even taking a play off, he always remembers *Hard Work Beats Talent When Talent Fails to Work Hard*.

For Kevin, it's simple.

"I want to be the best player ever. That's what drives me."

LEBRON JAMES

LeBron James's early years were not the easiest. When he was three, his grandmother, who was helping to raise him, passed away. His mother, Gloria James, had to bring him up alone without any help. To find work, she and LeBron moved 12 times in one three-year span, from ages five to eight.

Constantly changing schools was hard for LeBron. As soon as he made friends, he would move again. At age nine, the moving finally stopped. LeBron settled into school and discovered sports.

At first, football was his favorite. But he liked to play basketball, too. When LeBron was 11, he and his youth basketball team (the Shooting Stars) played in an Amateur Athletic Union tournament in Florida. The Shooting Stars finished ninth out of 64 teams in his age group. LeBron was hooked.

LeBron and his friends on the Shooting Stars continued to improve. By age 14, he stood 6-2 and already could dunk the basketball. His favorite part of the game, though, was delivering a pass to a teammate for an easy score. Then, as now, he was a team-first player.

LeBron and his three friends—Sian Cotton, Little Dru Joyce, and Willie McGee—stuck together. They all chose the same high school, St. Vincent-St. Mary. Athletically, St. V was known for being a football school. It had never had much success in hoops. That was about to change.

In four seasons, LeBron and his teammates won three state titles. LeBron went from being a skinny kid to a 6-8 powerhouse who looked like a man among boys on the basketball court. In his senior year, one national poll ranked St. V as the top high-school basketball team in the country. LeBron's games were televised locally, and he appeared on the cover of *Sports Illustrated* with the headline, "The Chosen One."

Not surprisingly, LeBron faced enormous expectations when he entered the NBA in 2003. But he has lived up to the challenge. In 2010, he joined the Miami Heat and quickly became one of their most valuable players. He had his most successful season ever in 2011–2012 when he won his third NBA MVP Award while averaging 27.1 points per game and making a career-best 53.1 percent of his field-goal attempts. In the 2012 NBA Playoffs, LeBron averaged 30.3 points, 9.7 rebounds, and 5.6 assists per game to lead

Miami to the NBA title, his first championship.

"It was a journey for myself," LeBron said after receiving the 2012 NBA Finals MVP Award. "Everything that went along with me being a high-school prodigy, when I was 16 on the cover of *Sports Illustrated*, to being drafted and having to be the face of a franchise . . . No one went through that journey, so I had to learn it on my own.

"I can finally say that I'm a champion, and I did it the right way. I didn't shortcut anything."

Growing up in Atlanta, Georgia, Dwight Howard dreamed of playing guard in the NBA. He certainly had the talent. By age 12 he could handle the ball equally well with his left or right hand. He was a terrific passer and an unselfish player who would do anything to help his team win.

Dwight loved to play basketball. He always smiled a little wider whenever he was on the court. In fact, he enjoyed basketball so much that he wrote a list of eight goals he wanted to achieve, and being picked number one in the NBA Draft was at the top.

Then, between ninth and tenth grade, Dwight grew. A lot. During the summer, he sprouted nearly half a foot, to 6-7 tall. The spurt did not end. By his senior year, he was nearly seven feet.

Dwight's height, strength, and skills made him a perfect power forward. He led his high-school team to a state title in 2004, and became a star before he turned 18.

All that attention did not change Dwight, though. He still did his chores and his homework. And he treated everyone with respect, just as his parents had taught him. "My mom and dad really laid a great foundation for me," he said.

Dwight also impressed NBA scouts with his drive and work ethic. Because he wanted to get stronger so he couldn't be pushed around on the court, he woke up every day at 5 a.m. to lift weights. After school, he practiced endlessly to develop his basketball skills.

All that extra effort paid off when the Orlando Magic selected him with the first pick in the 2004 NBA Draft. His dream had become reality, though many fans questioned the Magic's decision. Dwight quickly won over the doubters, and during his eight seasons in Orlando, he became the NBA's top center. He had his best season in 2010–2011, finishing second in the voting for the NBA Most Valuable Player Award while winning his third consecutive NBA Defensive Player of the Year Award.

"I think I've gotten a little bit better every year, but this has been

my best year as far as having more complete games," Dwight said in 2011. "I feel like I've been more consistent than ever on both ends [offense and defense]."

After a back injury shortened his 2011–2012 season, Dwight found a new home when Orlando traded him to Los Angeles in the summer of 2012. The Lakers believed Dwight would extend a tradition of great centers that includes George Mikan, Wilt Chamberlain, Kareem Abdul-Jabbar, and Shaquille O'Neal.

"I don't want to try to compete with those guys," Dwight said. "I want to bring my own flavor to L.A. . . . I want to be great in my own right. I want to write my own history and today is the first day of that history."

CARMELO ANTHONY

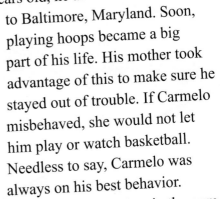

In 2011, Carmelo Anthony came home. "I feel like I'm still dreaming right now," said Carmelo after he joined the Knicks in February 2011. The trade that brought him to New York involved 13 players and three teams. But the Knicks knew Carmelo was worth it.

He scored 27 points in his Knicks debut, leading New York to a 114-108 win over Milwaukee. His late dunk and clutch free throws with 11.4 seconds left helped secure the victory, leading the Knicks fans to chant "Melo!" as the clock wound down.

For Carmelo, who was born in Brooklyn, there was nowhere else he'd rather be. When he was younger, Carmelo especially looked forward to spring in the city when he could watch the NCAA Tournament and the NBA Playoffs.

When Carmelo was eight years old, he and his mother moved to Baltimore, Maryland. Soon, playing hoops became a big part of his life. His mother took advantage of this to make sure he stayed out of trouble. If Carmelo misbehaved, she would not let him play or watch basketball. Needless to say, Carmelo was always on his best behavior.

All Carmelo's time in the gym made him a great ball-handler. But his lack of size prevented him from making his high school team as a freshman. He grew five inches before his sophomore year, and soon he was a 6-8 forward who could handle the ball like a guard. By his junior year, colleges were lining up to recruit him.

He chose Syracuse, although the Orangemen's coach, Jim Boeheim, doubted Carmelo could help immediately. "He wasn't a top 40 player when I recruited him," Boeheim said. "He was 170 pounds."

But Carmelo hit the gym, built muscle, bulked up, and arrived at Syracuse weighing 220 pounds. He became a starter immediately and proceeded to put together one of the greatest seasons ever by a freshman. Carmelo capped the year by leading Syracuse to its first title with an 81-78 victory over Kansas in the 2003 NCAA Championship Game. Carmelo had 20 points, 10 rebounds, and seven assists.

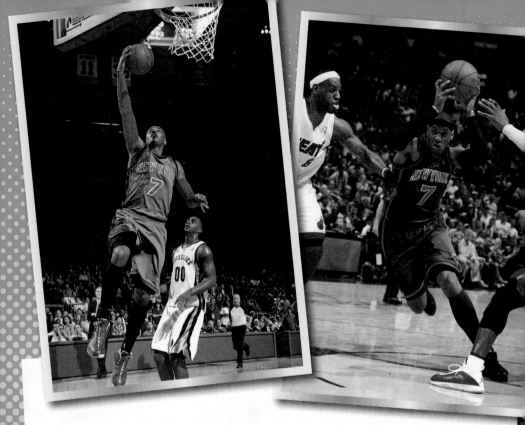

"We never talked about him being the best freshman in the country," Boeheim said after the victory over Kansas. "We talked about him being the best *player* in the country. I think in this tournament he proved it."

Carmelo has gone on to become one of the strongest players in the world. He averaged nearly 25 points per game during his first nine seasons in the NBA, leading his team to the NBA Playoffs each season (seven times with the Denver Nuggets and twice with the New York Knicks).

But despite all of Carmelo's success, Knicks fans expect even *more* from him. They expect a title. And Carmelo is ready to go.

"I'm sitting here in one of the best places in the world," Carmelo said the day of the trade. "It takes a certain kind of person to be able to do it in New York City, and I'm willing to accept those challenges."